Date: Time:

Caller:

Company:

Phone:

Email:

Urgency: Low/Medium/High

Message:

Called ☐

Date: Time:

Caller:

Company:

Phone:

Email:

Urgency: Low/Medium/High

Message:

Called ☐

Date: Time:

Caller:

Company:

Phone:

Email:

Urgency: Low/Medium/High

Message:

Called ☐

Date: Time:

Caller:

Company:

Phone:

Email:

Urgency: Low/Medium/High

Message:

Called ☐

Date: Time:

Caller:

Company:

Phone:

Email:

Urgency: Low/Medium/High

Message:

Called ☐

Date: Time:	Message:
Caller:	
Company:	
Phone:	
Email:	
Urgency: Low/Medium/High	Called ☐
Date: Time:	Message:
Caller:	
Company:	
Phone:	
Email:	
Urgency: Low/Medium/High	Called ☐
Date: Time:	Message:
Caller:	
Company:	
Phone:	
Email:	
Urgency: Low/Medium/High	Called ☐
Date: Time:	Message:
Caller:	
Company:	
Phone:	
Email:	
Urgency: Low/Medium/High	Called ☐
Date: Time:	Message:
Caller:	
Company:	
Phone:	
Email:	
Urgency: Low/Medium/High	Called ☐

Date: Time:	Message:
Caller:	
Company:	
Phone:	
Email:	
Urgency: Low/Medium/High	Called ☐
Date: Time:	Message:
Caller:	
Company:	
Phone:	
Email:	
Urgency: Low/Medium/High	Called ☐
Date: Time:	Message:
Caller:	
Company:	
Phone:	
Email:	
Urgency: Low/Medium/High	Called ☐
Date: Time:	Message:
Caller:	
Company:	
Phone:	
Email:	
Urgency: Low/Medium/High	Called ☐
Date: Time:	Message:
Caller:	
Company:	
Phone:	
Email:	
Urgency: Low/Medium/High	Called ☐

Date: Time:	Message:
Caller:	
Company:	
Phone:	
Email:	
Urgency: Low/Medium/High	Called ☐
Date: Time:	Message:
Caller:	
Company:	
Phone:	
Email:	
Urgency: Low/Medium/High	Called ☐
Date: Time:	Message:
Caller:	
Company:	
Phone:	
Email:	
Urgency: Low/Medium/High	Called ☐
Date: Time:	Message:
Caller:	
Company:	
Phone:	
Email:	
Urgency: Low/Medium/High	Called ☐
Date: Time:	Message:
Caller:	
Company:	
Phone:	
Email:	
Urgency: Low/Medium/High	Called ☐

	Message:
Date: Time:	
Caller:	
Company:	
Phone:	
Email:	
Urgency: Low/Medium/High	Called ☐
Date: Time:	Message:
Caller:	
Company:	
Phone:	
Email:	
Urgency: Low/Medium/High	Called ☐
Date: Time:	Message:
Caller:	
Company:	
Phone:	
Email:	
Urgency: Low/Medium/High	Called ☐
Date: Time:	Message:
Caller:	
Company:	
Phone:	
Email:	
Urgency: Low/Medium/High	Called ☐
Date: Time:	Message:
Caller:	
Company:	
Phone:	
Email:	
Urgency: Low/Medium/High	Called ☐

Date: Time:	Message:
Caller:	
Company:	
Phone:	
Email:	
Urgency: Low/Medium/High	Called ☐
Date: Time:	Message:
Caller:	
Company:	
Phone:	
Email:	
Urgency: Low/Medium/High	Called ☐
Date: Time:	Message:
Caller:	
Company:	
Phone:	
Email:	
Urgency: Low/Medium/High	Called ☐
Date: Time:	Message:
Caller:	
Company:	
Phone:	
Email:	
Urgency: Low/Medium/High	Called ☐
Date: Time:	Message:
Caller:	
Company:	
Phone:	
Email:	
Urgency: Low/Medium/High	Called ☐

	Message:
Date: Time:	
Caller:	
Company:	
Phone:	
Email:	
Urgency: Low/Medium/High	Called ☐
Date: Time:	Message:
Caller:	
Company:	
Phone:	
Email:	
Urgency: Low/Medium/High	Called ☐
Date: Time:	Message:
Caller:	
Company:	
Phone:	
Email:	
Urgency: Low/Medium/High	Called ☐
Date: Time:	Message:
Caller:	
Company:	
Phone:	
Email:	
Urgency: Low/Medium/High	Called ☐
Date: Time:	Message:
Caller:	
Company:	
Phone:	
Email:	
Urgency: Low/Medium/High	Called ☐

Date: Time:	Message:
Caller:	
Company:	
Phone:	
Email:	
Urgency: Low/Medium/High	Called ☐
Date: Time:	Message:
Caller:	
Company:	
Phone:	
Email:	
Urgency: Low/Medium/High	Called ☐
Date: Time:	Message:
Caller:	
Company:	
Phone:	
Email:	
Urgency: Low/Medium/High	Called ☐
Date: Time:	Message:
Caller:	
Company:	
Phone:	
Email:	
Urgency: Low/Medium/High	Called ☐
Date: Time:	Message:
Caller:	
Company:	
Phone:	
Email:	
Urgency: Low/Medium/High	Called ☐

Date: Time:	Message:
Caller:	
Company:	
Phone:	
Email:	
Urgency: Low/Medium/High	Called ☐
Date: Time:	Message:
Caller:	
Company:	
Phone:	
Email:	
Urgency: Low/Medium/High	Called ☐
Date: Time:	Message:
Caller:	
Company:	
Phone:	
Email:	
Urgency: Low/Medium/High	Called ☐
Date: Time:	Message:
Caller:	
Company:	
Phone:	
Email:	
Urgency: Low/Medium/High	Called ☐
Date: Time:	Message:
Caller:	
Company:	
Phone:	
Email:	
Urgency: Low/Medium/High	Called ☐

Date: Time:	Message:
Caller:	
Company:	
Phone:	
Email:	
Urgency: Low/Medium/High	Called ☐
Date: Time:	Message:
Caller:	
Company:	
Phone:	
Email:	
Urgency: Low/Medium/High	Called ☐
Date: Time:	Message:
Caller:	
Company:	
Phone:	
Email:	
Urgency: Low/Medium/High	Called ☐
Date: Time:	Message:
Caller:	
Company:	
Phone:	
Email:	
Urgency: Low/Medium/High	Called ☐
Date: Time:	Message:
Caller:	
Company:	
Phone:	
Email:	
Urgency: Low/Medium/High	Called ☐

Date: Time:	Message:
Caller:	
Company:	
Phone:	
Email:	
Urgency: Low/Medium/High	Called ☐
Date: Time:	Message:
Caller:	
Company:	
Phone:	
Email:	
Urgency: Low/Medium/High	Called ☐
Date: Time:	Message:
Caller:	
Company:	
Phone:	
Email:	
Urgency: Low/Medium/High	Called ☐
Date: Time:	Message:
Caller:	
Company:	
Phone:	
Email:	
Urgency: Low/Medium/High	Called ☐
Date: Time:	Message:
Caller:	
Company:	
Phone:	
Email:	
Urgency: Low/Medium/High	Called ☐

	Message:
Date: Time:	
Caller:	
Company:	
Phone:	
Email:	
Urgency: Low/Medium/High	Called ☐
Date: Time:	Message:
Caller:	
Company:	
Phone:	
Email:	
Urgency: Low/Medium/High	Called ☐
Date: Time:	Message:
Caller:	
Company:	
Phone:	
Email:	
Urgency: Low/Medium/High	Called ☐
Date: Time:	Message:
Caller:	
Company:	
Phone:	
Email:	
Urgency: Low/Medium/High	Called ☐
Date: Time:	Message:
Caller:	
Company:	
Phone:	
Email:	
Urgency: Low/Medium/High	Called ☐

Date: Time:	Message:
Caller:	
Company:	
Phone:	
Email:	
Urgency: Low/Medium/High	Called ☐
Date: Time:	Message:
Caller:	
Company:	
Phone:	
Email:	
Urgency: Low/Medium/High	Called ☐
Date: Time:	Message:
Caller:	
Company:	
Phone:	
Email:	
Urgency: Low/Medium/High	Called ☐
Date: Time:	Message:
Caller:	
Company:	
Phone:	
Email:	
Urgency: Low/Medium/High	Called ☐
Date: Time:	Message:
Caller:	
Company:	
Phone:	
Email:	
Urgency: Low/Medium/High	Called ☐

	Message:
Date: Time:	
Caller:	
Company:	
Phone:	
Email:	
Urgency: Low/Medium/High	Called ☐
Date: Time:	Message:
Caller:	
Company:	
Phone:	
Email:	
Urgency: Low/Medium/High	Called ☐
Date: Time:	Message:
Caller:	
Company:	
Phone:	
Email:	
Urgency: Low/Medium/High	Called ☐
Date: Time:	Message:
Caller:	
Company:	
Phone:	
Email:	
Urgency: Low/Medium/High	Called ☐
Date: Time:	Message:
Caller:	
Company:	
Phone:	
Email:	
Urgency: Low/Medium/High	Called ☐

	Message:
Date: Time:	
Caller:	
Company:	
Phone:	
Email:	
Urgency: Low/Medium/High	Called ☐
Date: Time:	Message:
Caller:	
Company:	
Phone:	
Email:	
Urgency: Low/Medium/High	Called ☐
Date: Time:	Message:
Caller:	
Company:	
Phone:	
Email:	
Urgency: Low/Medium/High	Called ☐
Date: Time:	Message:
Caller:	
Company:	
Phone:	
Email:	
Urgency: Low/Medium/High	Called ☐
Date: Time:	Message:
Caller:	
Company:	
Phone:	
Email:	
Urgency: Low/Medium/High	Called ☐

	Message:
Date: Time:	
Caller:	
Company:	
Phone:	
Email:	
Urgency: Low/Medium/High	Called ☐
Date: Time:	Message:
Caller:	
Company:	
Phone:	
Email:	
Urgency: Low/Medium/High	Called ☐
Date: Time:	Message:
Caller:	
Company:	
Phone:	
Email:	
Urgency: Low/Medium/High	Called ☐
Date: Time:	Message:
Caller:	
Company:	
Phone:	
Email:	
Urgency: Low/Medium/High	Called ☐
Date: Time:	Message:
Caller:	
Company:	
Phone:	
Email:	
Urgency: Low/Medium/High	Called ☐

Date:	Time:	Message:
Caller:		
Company:		
Phone:		
Email:		
Urgency: Low/Medium/High		Called ☐
Date:	Time:	Message:
Caller:		
Company:		
Phone:		
Email:		
Urgency: Low/Medium/High		Called ☐
Date:	Time:	Message:
Caller:		
Company:		
Phone:		
Email:		
Urgency: Low/Medium/High		Called ☐
Date:	Time:	Message:
Caller:		
Company:		
Phone:		
Email:		
Urgency: Low/Medium/High		Called ☐
Date:	Time:	Message:
Caller:		
Company:		
Phone:		
Email:		
Urgency: Low/Medium/High		Called ☐

Date: Time:	Message:
Caller:	
Company:	
Phone:	
Email:	
Urgency: Low/Medium/High	Called ☐
Date: Time:	Message:
Caller:	
Company:	
Phone:	
Email:	
Urgency: Low/Medium/High	Called ☐
Date: Time:	Message:
Caller:	
Company:	
Phone:	
Email:	
Urgency: Low/Medium/High	Called ☐
Date: Time:	Message:
Caller:	
Company:	
Phone:	
Email:	
Urgency: Low/Medium/High	Called ☐
Date: Time:	Message:
Caller:	
Company:	
Phone:	
Email:	
Urgency: Low/Medium/High	Called ☐

Date: Time:	Message:
Caller:	
Company:	
Phone:	
Email:	
Urgency: Low/Medium/High	Called ☐
Date: Time:	Message:
Caller:	
Company:	
Phone:	
Email:	
Urgency: Low/Medium/High	Called ☐
Date: Time:	Message:
Caller:	
Company:	
Phone:	
Email:	
Urgency: Low/Medium/High	Called ☐
Date: Time:	Message:
Caller:	
Company:	
Phone:	
Email:	
Urgency: Low/Medium/High	Called ☐
Date: Time:	Message:
Caller:	
Company:	
Phone:	
Email:	
Urgency: Low/Medium/High	Called ☐

Date: Time:	Message:
Caller:	
Company:	
Phone:	
Email:	
Urgency: Low/Medium/High	Called ☐
Date: Time:	Message:
Caller:	
Company:	
Phone:	
Email:	
Urgency: Low/Medium/High	Called ☐
Date: Time:	Message:
Caller:	
Company:	
Phone:	
Email:	
Urgency: Low/Medium/High	Called ☐
Date: Time:	Message:
Caller:	
Company:	
Phone:	
Email:	
Urgency: Low/Medium/High	Called ☐
Date: Time:	Message:
Caller:	
Company:	
Phone:	
Email:	
Urgency: Low/Medium/High	Called ☐

Date: Time:	Message:
Caller:	
Company:	
Phone:	
Email:	
Urgency: Low/Medium/High	Called ☐
Date: Time:	Message:
Caller:	
Company:	
Phone:	
Email:	
Urgency: Low/Medium/High	Called ☐
Date: Time:	Message:
Caller:	
Company:	
Phone:	
Email:	
Urgency: Low/Medium/High	Called ☐
Date: Time:	Message:
Caller:	
Company:	
Phone:	
Email:	
Urgency: Low/Medium/High	Called ☐
Date: Time:	Message:
Caller:	
Company:	
Phone:	
Email:	
Urgency: Low/Medium/High	Called ☐

	Message:
Date: Time:	
Caller:	
Company:	
Phone:	
Email:	
Urgency: Low/Medium/High	Called ☐
Date: Time:	Message:
Caller:	
Company:	
Phone:	
Email:	
Urgency: Low/Medium/High	Called ☐
Date: Time:	Message:
Caller:	
Company:	
Phone:	
Email:	
Urgency: Low/Medium/High	Called ☐
Date: Time:	Message:
Caller:	
Company:	
Phone:	
Email:	
Urgency: Low/Medium/High	Called ☐
Date: Time:	Message:
Caller:	
Company:	
Phone:	
Email:	
Urgency: Low/Medium/High	Called ☐

Date: Time:	Message:
Caller:	
Company:	
Phone:	
Email:	
Urgency: Low/Medium/High	Called ☐
Date: Time:	Message:
Caller:	
Company:	
Phone:	
Email:	
Urgency: Low/Medium/High	Called ☐
Date: Time:	Message:
Caller:	
Company:	
Phone:	
Email:	
Urgency: Low/Medium/High	Called ☐
Date: Time:	Message:
Caller:	
Company:	
Phone:	
Email:	
Urgency: Low/Medium/High	Called ☐
Date: Time:	Message:
Caller:	
Company:	
Phone:	
Email:	
Urgency: Low/Medium/High	Called ☐

Date: Time:	Message:
Caller:	
Company:	
Phone:	
Email:	
Urgency: Low/Medium/High	Called ☐
Date: Time:	Message:
Caller:	
Company:	
Phone:	
Email:	
Urgency: Low/Medium/High	Called ☐
Date: Time:	Message:
Caller:	
Company:	
Phone:	
Email:	
Urgency: Low/Medium/High	Called ☐
Date: Time:	Message:
Caller:	
Company:	
Phone:	
Email:	
Urgency: Low/Medium/High	Called ☐
Date: Time:	Message:
Caller:	
Company:	
Phone:	
Email:	
Urgency: Low/Medium/High	Called ☐

Date: Time:	Message:
Caller:	
Company:	
Phone:	
Email:	
Urgency: Low/Medium/High	Called ☐
Date: Time:	Message:
Caller:	
Company:	
Phone:	
Email:	
Urgency: Low/Medium/High	Called ☐
Date: Time:	Message:
Caller:	
Company:	
Phone:	
Email:	
Urgency: Low/Medium/High	Called ☐
Date: Time:	Message:
Caller:	
Company:	
Phone:	
Email:	
Urgency: Low/Medium/High	Called ☐
Date: Time:	Message:
Caller:	
Company:	
Phone:	
Email:	
Urgency: Low/Medium/High	Called ☐

Date: Time:	Message:
Caller:	
Company:	
Phone:	
Email:	
Urgency: Low/Medium/High	Called ☐
Date: Time:	Message:
Caller:	
Company:	
Phone:	
Email:	
Urgency: Low/Medium/High	Called ☐
Date: Time:	Message:
Caller:	
Company:	
Phone:	
Email:	
Urgency: Low/Medium/High	Called ☐
Date: Time:	Message:
Caller:	
Company:	
Phone:	
Email:	
Urgency: Low/Medium/High	Called ☐
Date: Time:	Message:
Caller:	
Company:	
Phone:	
Email:	
Urgency: Low/Medium/High	Called ☐

	Message:
Date: Time:	
Caller:	
Company:	
Phone:	
Email:	
Urgency: Low/Medium/High	Called ☐
Date: Time:	Message:
Caller:	
Company:	
Phone:	
Email:	
Urgency: Low/Medium/High	Called ☐
Date: Time:	Message:
Caller:	
Company:	
Phone:	
Email:	
Urgency: Low/Medium/High	Called ☐
Date: Time:	Message:
Caller:	
Company:	
Phone:	
Email:	
Urgency: Low/Medium/High	Called ☐
Date: Time:	Message:
Caller:	
Company:	
Phone:	
Email:	
Urgency: Low/Medium/High	Called ☐

Date:　　　　　　Time:	Message:
Caller:	
Company:	
Phone:	
Email:	
Urgency: Low/Medium/High	Called ☐
Date:　　　　　　Time:	Message:
Caller:	
Company:	
Phone:	
Email:	
Urgency: Low/Medium/High	Called ☐
Date:　　　　　　Time:	Message:
Caller:	
Company:	
Phone:	
Email:	
Urgency: Low/Medium/High	Called ☐
Date:　　　　　　Time:	Message:
Caller:	
Company:	
Phone:	
Email:	
Urgency: Low/Medium/High	Called ☐
Date:　　　　　　Time:	Message:
Caller:	
Company:	
Phone:	
Email:	
Urgency: Low/Medium/High	Called ☐

Date: Time:	Message:
Caller:	
Company:	
Phone:	
Email:	
Urgency: Low/Medium/High	Called ☐
Date: Time:	Message:
Caller:	
Company:	
Phone:	
Email:	
Urgency: Low/Medium/High	Called ☐
Date: Time:	Message:
Caller:	
Company:	
Phone:	
Email:	
Urgency: Low/Medium/High	Called ☐
Date: Time:	Message:
Caller:	
Company:	
Phone:	
Email:	
Urgency: Low/Medium/High	Called ☐
Date: Time:	Message:
Caller:	
Company:	
Phone:	
Email:	
Urgency: Low/Medium/High	Called ☐

	Message:
Date: Time:	
Caller:	
Company:	
Phone:	
Email:	
Urgency: Low/Medium/High	Called ☐

	Message:
Date: Time:	
Caller:	
Company:	
Phone:	
Email:	
Urgency: Low/Medium/High	Called ☐

	Message:
Date: Time:	
Caller:	
Company:	
Phone:	
Email:	
Urgency: Low/Medium/High	Called ☐

	Message:
Date: Time:	
Caller:	
Company:	
Phone:	
Email:	
Urgency: Low/Medium/High	Called ☐

	Message:
Date: Time:	
Caller:	
Company:	
Phone:	
Email:	
Urgency: Low/Medium/High	Called ☐

Date: Time:	Message:
Caller:	
Company:	
Phone:	
Email:	
Urgency: Low/Medium/High	Called ☐
Date: Time:	Message:
Caller:	
Company:	
Phone:	
Email:	
Urgency: Low/Medium/High	Called ☐
Date: Time:	Message:
Caller:	
Company:	
Phone:	
Email:	
Urgency: Low/Medium/High	Called ☐
Date: Time:	Message:
Caller:	
Company:	
Phone:	
Email:	
Urgency: Low/Medium/High	Called ☐
Date: Time:	Message:
Caller:	
Company:	
Phone:	
Email:	
Urgency: Low/Medium/High	Called ☐

Date: Time:	Message:
Caller:	
Company:	
Phone:	
Email:	
Urgency: Low/Medium/High	Called ☐
Date: Time:	Message:
Caller:	
Company:	
Phone:	
Email:	
Urgency: Low/Medium/High	Called ☐
Date: Time:	Message:
Caller:	
Company:	
Phone:	
Email:	
Urgency: Low/Medium/High	Called ☐
Date: Time:	Message:
Caller:	
Company:	
Phone:	
Email:	
Urgency: Low/Medium/High	Called ☐
Date: Time:	Message:
Caller:	
Company:	
Phone:	
Email:	
Urgency: Low/Medium/High	Called ☐

	Message:
Date: Time:	
Caller:	
Company:	
Phone:	
Email:	
Urgency: Low/Medium/High	Called ☐
Date: Time:	Message:
Caller:	
Company:	
Phone:	
Email:	
Urgency: Low/Medium/High	Called ☐
Date: Time:	Message:
Caller:	
Company:	
Phone:	
Email:	
Urgency: Low/Medium/High	Called ☐
Date: Time:	Message:
Caller:	
Company:	
Phone:	
Email:	
Urgency: Low/Medium/High	Called ☐
Date: Time:	Message:
Caller:	
Company:	
Phone:	
Email:	
Urgency: Low/Medium/High	Called ☐

	Message:
Date: Time:	
Caller:	
Company:	
Phone:	
Email:	
Urgency: Low/Medium/High	Called ☐
Date: Time:	Message:
Caller:	
Company:	
Phone:	
Email:	
Urgency: Low/Medium/High	Called ☐
Date: Time:	Message:
Caller:	
Company:	
Phone:	
Email:	
Urgency: Low/Medium/High	Called ☐
Date: Time:	Message:
Caller:	
Company:	
Phone:	
Email:	
Urgency: Low/Medium/High	Called ☐
Date: Time:	Message:
Caller:	
Company:	
Phone:	
Email:	
Urgency: Low/Medium/High	Called ☐

Date: Time:	Message:
Caller:	
Company:	
Phone:	
Email:	
Urgency: Low/Medium/High	Called ☐
Date: Time:	Message:
Caller:	
Company:	
Phone:	
Email:	
Urgency: Low/Medium/High	Called ☐
Date: Time:	Message:
Caller:	
Company:	
Phone:	
Email:	
Urgency: Low/Medium/High	Called ☐
Date: Time:	Message:
Caller:	
Company:	
Phone:	
Email:	
Urgency: Low/Medium/High	Called ☐
Date: Time:	Message:
Caller:	
Company:	
Phone:	
Email:	
Urgency: Low/Medium/High	Called ☐

Date: Time:	Message:
Caller:	
Company:	
Phone:	
Email:	
Urgency: Low/Medium/High	Called ☐
Date: Time:	Message:
Caller:	
Company:	
Phone:	
Email:	
Urgency: Low/Medium/High	Called ☐
Date: Time:	Message:
Caller:	
Company:	
Phone:	
Email:	
Urgency: Low/Medium/High	Called ☐
Date: Time:	Message:
Caller:	
Company:	
Phone:	
Email:	
Urgency: Low/Medium/High	Called ☐
Date: Time:	Message:
Caller:	
Company:	
Phone:	
Email:	
Urgency: Low/Medium/High	Called ☐

Date: Time:	Message:
Caller:	
Company:	
Phone:	
Email:	
Urgency: Low/Medium/High	Called ☐
Date: Time:	Message:
Caller:	
Company:	
Phone:	
Email:	
Urgency: Low/Medium/High	Called ☐
Date: Time:	Message:
Caller:	
Company:	
Phone:	
Email:	
Urgency: Low/Medium/High	Called ☐
Date: Time:	Message:
Caller:	
Company:	
Phone:	
Email:	
Urgency: Low/Medium/High	Called ☐
Date: Time:	Message:
Caller:	
Company:	
Phone:	
Email:	
Urgency: Low/Medium/High	Called ☐

	Message:
Date: Time:	
Caller:	
Company:	
Phone:	
Email:	
Urgency: Low/Medium/High	Called ☐

	Message:
Date: Time:	
Caller:	
Company:	
Phone:	
Email:	
Urgency: Low/Medium/High	Called ☐

	Message:
Date: Time:	
Caller:	
Company:	
Phone:	
Email:	
Urgency: Low/Medium/High	Called ☐

	Message:
Date: Time:	
Caller:	
Company:	
Phone:	
Email:	
Urgency: Low/Medium/High	Called ☐

	Message:
Date: Time:	
Caller:	
Company:	
Phone:	
Email:	
Urgency: Low/Medium/High	Called ☐

Date: Time:	Message:
Caller:	
Company:	
Phone:	
Email:	
Urgency: Low/Medium/High	Called ☐
Date: Time:	Message:
Caller:	
Company:	
Phone:	
Email:	
Urgency: Low/Medium/High	Called ☐
Date: Time:	Message:
Caller:	
Company:	
Phone:	
Email:	
Urgency: Low/Medium/High	Called ☐
Date: Time:	Message:
Caller:	
Company:	
Phone:	
Email:	
Urgency: Low/Medium/High	Called ☐
Date: Time:	Message:
Caller:	
Company:	
Phone:	
Email:	
Urgency: Low/Medium/High	Called ☐

	Message:
Date: Time:	
Caller:	
Company:	
Phone:	
Email:	
Urgency: Low/Medium/High	Called ☐
Date: Time:	Message:
Caller:	
Company:	
Phone:	
Email:	
Urgency: Low/Medium/High	Called ☐
Date: Time:	Message:
Caller:	
Company:	
Phone:	
Email:	
Urgency: Low/Medium/High	Called ☐
Date: Time:	Message:
Caller:	
Company:	
Phone:	
Email:	
Urgency: Low/Medium/High	Called ☐
Date: Time:	Message:
Caller:	
Company:	
Phone:	
Email:	
Urgency: Low/Medium/High	Called ☐

	Message:
Date: Time:	
Caller:	
Company:	
Phone:	
Email:	
Urgency: Low/Medium/High	Called ☐
Date: Time:	Message:
Caller:	
Company:	
Phone:	
Email:	
Urgency: Low/Medium/High	Called ☐
Date: Time:	Message:
Caller:	
Company:	
Phone:	
Email:	
Urgency: Low/Medium/High	Called ☐
Date: Time:	Message:
Caller:	
Company:	
Phone:	
Email:	
Urgency: Low/Medium/High	Called ☐
Date: Time:	Message:
Caller:	
Company:	
Phone:	
Email:	
Urgency: Low/Medium/High	Called ☐

	Message:
Date: Time:	
Caller:	
Company:	
Phone:	
Email:	
Urgency: Low/Medium/High	Called ☐
Date: Time:	Message:
Caller:	
Company:	
Phone:	
Email:	
Urgency: Low/Medium/High	Called ☐
Date: Time:	Message:
Caller:	
Company:	
Phone:	
Email:	
Urgency: Low/Medium/High	Called ☐
Date: Time:	Message:
Caller:	
Company:	
Phone:	
Email:	
Urgency: Low/Medium/High	Called ☐
Date: Time:	Message:
Caller:	
Company:	
Phone:	
Email:	
Urgency: Low/Medium/High	Called ☐

Date: Time:	Message:
Caller:	
Company:	
Phone:	
Email:	
Urgency: Low/Medium/High	Called ☐
Date: Time:	Message:
Caller:	
Company:	
Phone:	
Email:	
Urgency: Low/Medium/High	Called ☐
Date: Time:	Message:
Caller:	
Company:	
Phone:	
Email:	
Urgency: Low/Medium/High	Called ☐
Date: Time:	Message:
Caller:	
Company:	
Phone:	
Email:	
Urgency: Low/Medium/High	Called ☐
Date: Time:	Message:
Caller:	
Company:	
Phone:	
Email:	
Urgency: Low/Medium/High	Called ☐

Date:　　　　　Time:	Message:
Caller:	
Company:	
Phone:	
Email:	
Urgency: Low/Medium/High	Called ☐
Date:　　　　　Time:	Message:
Caller:	
Company:	
Phone:	
Email:	
Urgency: Low/Medium/High	Called ☐
Date:　　　　　Time:	Message:
Caller:	
Company:	
Phone:	
Email:	
Urgency: Low/Medium/High	Called ☐
Date:　　　　　Time:	Message:
Caller:	
Company:	
Phone:	
Email:	
Urgency: Low/Medium/High	Called ☐
Date:　　　　　Time:	Message:
Caller:	
Company:	
Phone:	
Email:	
Urgency: Low/Medium/High	Called ☐

Date: Time:	Message:
Caller:	
Company:	
Phone:	
Email:	
Urgency: Low/Medium/High	Called ☐
Date: Time:	Message:
Caller:	
Company:	
Phone:	
Email:	
Urgency: Low/Medium/High	Called ☐
Date: Time:	Message:
Caller:	
Company:	
Phone:	
Email:	
Urgency: Low/Medium/High	Called ☐
Date: Time:	Message:
Caller:	
Company:	
Phone:	
Email:	
Urgency: Low/Medium/High	Called ☐
Date: Time:	Message:
Caller:	
Company:	
Phone:	
Email:	
Urgency: Low/Medium/High	Called ☐

	Message:
Date: Time:	
Caller:	
Company:	
Phone:	
Email:	
Urgency: Low/Medium/High	Called ☐
Date: Time:	Message:
Caller:	
Company:	
Phone:	
Email:	
Urgency: Low/Medium/High	Called ☐
Date: Time:	Message:
Caller:	
Company:	
Phone:	
Email:	
Urgency: Low/Medium/High	Called ☐
Date: Time:	Message:
Caller:	
Company:	
Phone:	
Email:	
Urgency: Low/Medium/High	Called ☐
Date: Time:	Message:
Caller:	
Company:	
Phone:	
Email:	
Urgency: Low/Medium/High	Called ☐

	Message:
Date: Time:	
Caller:	
Company:	
Phone:	
Email:	
Urgency: Low/Medium/High	Called ☐
Date: Time:	Message:
Caller:	
Company:	
Phone:	
Email:	
Urgency: Low/Medium/High	Called ☐
Date: Time:	Message:
Caller:	
Company:	
Phone:	
Email:	
Urgency: Low/Medium/High	Called ☐
Date: Time:	Message:
Caller:	
Company:	
Phone:	
Email:	
Urgency: Low/Medium/High	Called ☐
Date: Time:	Message:
Caller:	
Company:	
Phone:	
Email:	
Urgency: Low/Medium/High	Called ☐

	Message:
Date: Time:	
Caller:	
Company:	
Phone:	
Email:	
Urgency: Low/Medium/High	Called ☐
Date: Time:	Message:
Caller:	
Company:	
Phone:	
Email:	
Urgency: Low/Medium/High	Called ☐
Date: Time:	Message:
Caller:	
Company:	
Phone:	
Email:	
Urgency: Low/Medium/High	Called ☐
Date: Time:	Message:
Caller:	
Company:	
Phone:	
Email:	
Urgency: Low/Medium/High	Called ☐
Date: Time:	Message:
Caller:	
Company:	
Phone:	
Email:	
Urgency: Low/Medium/High	Called ☐

Date: Time:	Message:
Caller:	
Company:	
Phone:	
Email:	
Urgency: Low/Medium/High	Called ☐
Date: Time:	Message:
Caller:	
Company:	
Phone:	
Email:	
Urgency: Low/Medium/High	Called ☐
Date: Time:	Message:
Caller:	
Company:	
Phone:	
Email:	
Urgency: Low/Medium/High	Called ☐
Date: Time:	Message:
Caller:	
Company:	
Phone:	
Email:	
Urgency: Low/Medium/High	Called ☐
Date: Time:	Message:
Caller:	
Company:	
Phone:	
Email:	
Urgency: Low/Medium/High	Called ☐

Date: Time:	Message:
Caller:	
Company:	
Phone:	
Email:	
Urgency: Low/Medium/High	Called ☐
Date: Time:	Message:
Caller:	
Company:	
Phone:	
Email:	
Urgency: Low/Medium/High	Called ☐
Date: Time:	Message:
Caller:	
Company:	
Phone:	
Email:	
Urgency: Low/Medium/High	Called ☐
Date: Time:	Message:
Caller:	
Company:	
Phone:	
Email:	
Urgency: Low/Medium/High	Called ☐
Date: Time:	Message:
Caller:	
Company:	
Phone:	
Email:	
Urgency: Low/Medium/High	Called ☐

Date: Time:	Message:
Caller:	
Company:	
Phone:	
Email:	
Urgency: Low/Medium/High	Called ☐
Date: Time:	Message:
Caller:	
Company:	
Phone:	
Email:	
Urgency: Low/Medium/High	Called ☐
Date: Time:	Message:
Caller:	
Company:	
Phone:	
Email:	
Urgency: Low/Medium/High	Called ☐
Date: Time:	Message:
Caller:	
Company:	
Phone:	
Email:	
Urgency: Low/Medium/High	Called ☐
Date: Time:	Message:
Caller:	
Company:	
Phone:	
Email:	
Urgency: Low/Medium/High	Called ☐

Date: Time:	Message:
Caller:	
Company:	
Phone:	
Email:	
Urgency: Low/Medium/High	Called ☐
Date: Time:	Message:
Caller:	
Company:	
Phone:	
Email:	
Urgency: Low/Medium/High	Called ☐
Date: Time:	Message:
Caller:	
Company:	
Phone:	
Email:	
Urgency: Low/Medium/High	Called ☐
Date: Time:	Message:
Caller:	
Company:	
Phone:	
Email:	
Urgency: Low/Medium/High	Called ☐
Date: Time:	Message:
Caller:	
Company:	
Phone:	
Email:	
Urgency: Low/Medium/High	Called ☐

Date: Time:	Message:
Caller:	
Company:	
Phone:	
Email:	
Urgency: Low/Medium/High	Called ☐
Date: Time:	Message:
Caller:	
Company:	
Phone:	
Email:	
Urgency: Low/Medium/High	Called ☐
Date: Time:	Message:
Caller:	
Company:	
Phone:	
Email:	
Urgency: Low/Medium/High	Called ☐
Date: Time:	Message:
Caller:	
Company:	
Phone:	
Email:	
Urgency: Low/Medium/High	Called ☐
Date: Time:	Message:
Caller:	
Company:	
Phone:	
Email:	
Urgency: Low/Medium/High	Called ☐

	Message:
Date: Time:	
Caller:	
Company:	
Phone:	
Email:	
Urgency: Low/Medium/High	Called ☐
Date: Time:	Message:
Caller:	
Company:	
Phone:	
Email:	
Urgency: Low/Medium/High	Called ☐
Date: Time:	Message:
Caller:	
Company:	
Phone:	
Email:	
Urgency: Low/Medium/High	Called ☐
Date: Time:	Message:
Caller:	
Company:	
Phone:	
Email:	
Urgency: Low/Medium/High	Called ☐
Date: Time:	Message:
Caller:	
Company:	
Phone:	
Email:	
Urgency: Low/Medium/High	Called ☐

	Message:
Date: Time:	
Caller:	
Company:	
Phone:	
Email:	
Urgency: Low/Medium/High	Called ☐
Date: Time:	Message:
Caller:	
Company:	
Phone:	
Email:	
Urgency: Low/Medium/High	Called ☐
Date: Time:	Message:
Caller:	
Company:	
Phone:	
Email:	
Urgency: Low/Medium/High	Called ☐
Date: Time:	Message:
Caller:	
Company:	
Phone:	
Email:	
Urgency: Low/Medium/High	Called ☐
Date: Time:	Message:
Caller:	
Company:	
Phone:	
Email:	
Urgency: Low/Medium/High	Called ☐

Date: Time:	Message:
Caller:	
Company:	
Phone:	
Email:	
Urgency: Low/Medium/High	Called ☐
Date: Time:	Message:
Caller:	
Company:	
Phone:	
Email:	
Urgency: Low/Medium/High	Called ☐
Date: Time:	Message:
Caller:	
Company:	
Phone:	
Email:	
Urgency: Low/Medium/High	Called ☐
Date: Time:	Message:
Caller:	
Company:	
Phone:	
Email:	
Urgency: Low/Medium/High	Called ☐
Date: Time:	Message:
Caller:	
Company:	
Phone:	
Email:	
Urgency: Low/Medium/High	Called ☐

Date:	Time:	Message:
Caller:		
Company:		
Phone:		
Email:		
Urgency: Low/Medium/High		Called ☐

Date:	Time:	Message:
Caller:		
Company:		
Phone:		
Email:		
Urgency: Low/Medium/High		Called ☐

Date:	Time:	Message:
Caller:		
Company:		
Phone:		
Email:		
Urgency: Low/Medium/High		Called ☐

Date:	Time:	Message:
Caller:		
Company:		
Phone:		
Email:		
Urgency: Low/Medium/High		Called ☐

Date:	Time:	Message:
Caller:		
Company:		
Phone:		
Email:		
Urgency: Low/Medium/High		Called ☐

Date: Time:	Message:
Caller:	
Company:	
Phone:	
Email:	
Urgency: Low/Medium/High	Called ☐

Date: Time:	Message:
Caller:	
Company:	
Phone:	
Email:	
Urgency: Low/Medium/High	Called ☐

Date: Time:	Message:
Caller:	
Company:	
Phone:	
Email:	
Urgency: Low/Medium/High	Called ☐

Date: Time:	Message:
Caller:	
Company:	
Phone:	
Email:	
Urgency: Low/Medium/High	Called ☐

Date: Time:	Message:
Caller:	
Company:	
Phone:	
Email:	
Urgency: Low/Medium/High	Called ☐

Date:　　　　　Time:	Message:
Caller:	
Company:	
Phone:	
Email:	
Urgency: Low/Medium/High	Called ☐
Date:　　　　　Time:	Message:
Caller:	
Company:	
Phone:	
Email:	
Urgency: Low/Medium/High	Called ☐
Date:　　　　　Time:	Message:
Caller:	
Company:	
Phone:	
Email:	
Urgency: Low/Medium/High	Called ☐
Date:　　　　　Time:	Message:
Caller:	
Company:	
Phone:	
Email:	
Urgency: Low/Medium/High	Called ☐
Date:　　　　　Time:	Message:
Caller:	
Company:	
Phone:	
Email:	
Urgency: Low/Medium/High	Called ☐

	Message:
Date: Time:	
Caller:	
Company:	
Phone:	
Email:	
Urgency: Low/Medium/High	Called ☐
Date: Time:	Message:
Caller:	
Company:	
Phone:	
Email:	
Urgency: Low/Medium/High	Called ☐
Date: Time:	Message:
Caller:	
Company:	
Phone:	
Email:	
Urgency: Low/Medium/High	Called ☐
Date: Time:	Message:
Caller:	
Company:	
Phone:	
Email:	
Urgency: Low/Medium/High	Called ☐
Date: Time:	Message:
Caller:	
Company:	
Phone:	
Email:	
Urgency: Low/Medium/High	Called ☐

	Message:
Date: Time:	
Caller:	
Company:	
Phone:	
Email:	
Urgency: Low/Medium/High	Called ☐
Date: Time:	Message:
Caller:	
Company:	
Phone:	
Email:	
Urgency: Low/Medium/High	Called ☐
Date: Time:	Message:
Caller:	
Company:	
Phone:	
Email:	
Urgency: Low/Medium/High	Called ☐
Date: Time:	Message:
Caller:	
Company:	
Phone:	
Email:	
Urgency: Low/Medium/High	Called ☐
Date: Time:	Message:
Caller:	
Company:	
Phone:	
Email:	
Urgency: Low/Medium/High	Called ☐

	Message:
Date: Time:	
Caller:	
Company:	
Phone:	
Email:	
Urgency: Low/Medium/High	Called ☐
Date: Time:	Message:
Caller:	
Company:	
Phone:	
Email:	
Urgency: Low/Medium/High	Called ☐
Date: Time:	Message:
Caller:	
Company:	
Phone:	
Email:	
Urgency: Low/Medium/High	Called ☐
Date: Time:	Message:
Caller:	
Company:	
Phone:	
Email:	
Urgency: Low/Medium/High	Called ☐
Date: Time:	Message:
Caller:	
Company:	
Phone:	
Email:	
Urgency: Low/Medium/High	Called ☐

	Message:
Date: Time:	
Caller:	
Company:	
Phone:	
Email:	
Urgency: Low/Medium/High	Called ☐
Date: Time:	Message:
Caller:	
Company:	
Phone:	
Email:	
Urgency: Low/Medium/High	Called ☐
Date: Time:	Message:
Caller:	
Company:	
Phone:	
Email:	
Urgency: Low/Medium/High	Called ☐
Date: Time:	Message:
Caller:	
Company:	
Phone:	
Email:	
Urgency: Low/Medium/High	Called ☐
Date: Time:	Message:
Caller:	
Company:	
Phone:	
Email:	
Urgency: Low/Medium/High	Called ☐

	Message:
Date: Time:	
Caller:	
Company:	
Phone:	
Email:	
Urgency: Low/Medium/High	Called ☐
Date: Time:	Message:
Caller:	
Company:	
Phone:	
Email:	
Urgency: Low/Medium/High	Called ☐
Date: Time:	Message:
Caller:	
Company:	
Phone:	
Email:	
Urgency: Low/Medium/High	Called ☐
Date: Time:	Message:
Caller:	
Company:	
Phone:	
Email:	
Urgency: Low/Medium/High	Called ☐
Date: Time:	Message:
Caller:	
Company:	
Phone:	
Email:	
Urgency: Low/Medium/High	Called ☐

Date: Time:	Message:
Caller:	
Company:	
Phone:	
Email:	
Urgency: Low/Medium/High	Called ☐
Date: Time:	Message:
Caller:	
Company:	
Phone:	
Email:	
Urgency: Low/Medium/High	Called ☐
Date: Time:	Message:
Caller:	
Company:	
Phone:	
Email:	
Urgency: Low/Medium/High	Called ☐
Date: Time:	Message:
Caller:	
Company:	
Phone:	
Email:	
Urgency: Low/Medium/High	Called ☐
Date: Time:	Message:
Caller:	
Company:	
Phone:	
Email:	
Urgency: Low/Medium/High	Called ☐

Date: Time:	Message:
Caller:	
Company:	
Phone:	
Email:	
Urgency: Low/Medium/High	Called ☐
Date: Time:	Message:
Caller:	
Company:	
Phone:	
Email:	
Urgency: Low/Medium/High	Called ☐
Date: Time:	Message:
Caller:	
Company:	
Phone:	
Email:	
Urgency: Low/Medium/High	Called ☐
Date: Time:	Message:
Caller:	
Company:	
Phone:	
Email:	
Urgency: Low/Medium/High	Called ☐
Date: Time:	Message:
Caller:	
Company:	
Phone:	
Email:	
Urgency: Low/Medium/High	Called ☐

Date: Time:	Message:
Caller:	
Company:	
Phone:	
Email:	
Urgency: Low/Medium/High	Called ☐
Date: Time:	Message:
Caller:	
Company:	
Phone:	
Email:	
Urgency: Low/Medium/High	Called ☐
Date: Time:	Message:
Caller:	
Company:	
Phone:	
Email:	
Urgency: Low/Medium/High	Called ☐
Date: Time:	Message:
Caller:	
Company:	
Phone:	
Email:	
Urgency: Low/Medium/High	Called ☐
Date: Time:	Message:
Caller:	
Company:	
Phone:	
Email:	
Urgency: Low/Medium/High	Called ☐

	Message:
Date: Time:	
Caller:	
Company:	
Phone:	
Email:	
Urgency: Low/Medium/High	Called ☐
Date: Time:	Message:
Caller:	
Company:	
Phone:	
Email:	
Urgency: Low/Medium/High	Called ☐
Date: Time:	Message:
Caller:	
Company:	
Phone:	
Email:	
Urgency: Low/Medium/High	Called ☐
Date: Time:	Message:
Caller:	
Company:	
Phone:	
Email:	
Urgency: Low/Medium/High	Called ☐
Date: Time:	Message:
Caller:	
Company:	
Phone:	
Email:	
Urgency: Low/Medium/High	Called ☐

Date: Time:	Message:
Caller:	
Company:	
Phone:	
Email:	
Urgency: Low/Medium/High	Called ☐
Date: Time:	Message:
Caller:	
Company:	
Phone:	
Email:	
Urgency: Low/Medium/High	Called ☐
Date: Time:	Message:
Caller:	
Company:	
Phone:	
Email:	
Urgency: Low/Medium/High	Called ☐
Date: Time:	Message:
Caller:	
Company:	
Phone:	
Email:	
Urgency: Low/Medium/High	Called ☐
Date: Time:	Message:
Caller:	
Company:	
Phone:	
Email:	
Urgency: Low/Medium/High	Called ☐

	Message:
Date: Time:	
Caller:	
Company:	
Phone:	
Email:	
Urgency: Low/Medium/High	Called ☐
Date: Time:	Message:
Caller:	
Company:	
Phone:	
Email:	
Urgency: Low/Medium/High	Called ☐
Date: Time:	Message:
Caller:	
Company:	
Phone:	
Email:	
Urgency: Low/Medium/High	Called ☐
Date: Time:	Message:
Caller:	
Company:	
Phone:	
Email:	
Urgency: Low/Medium/High	Called ☐
Date: Time:	Message:
Caller:	
Company:	
Phone:	
Email:	
Urgency: Low/Medium/High	Called ☐

Date: Time:	Message:
Caller:	
Company:	
Phone:	
Email:	
Urgency: Low/Medium/High	Called ☐
Date: Time:	Message:
Caller:	
Company:	
Phone:	
Email:	
Urgency: Low/Medium/High	Called ☐
Date: Time:	Message:
Caller:	
Company:	
Phone:	
Email:	
Urgency: Low/Medium/High	Called ☐
Date: Time:	Message:
Caller:	
Company:	
Phone:	
Email:	
Urgency: Low/Medium/High	Called ☐
Date: Time:	Message:
Caller:	
Company:	
Phone:	
Email:	
Urgency: Low/Medium/High	Called ☐

	Message:
Date: Time:	
Caller:	
Company:	
Phone:	
Email:	
Urgency: Low/Medium/High	Called ☐
Date: Time:	Message:
Caller:	
Company:	
Phone:	
Email:	
Urgency: Low/Medium/High	Called ☐
Date: Time:	Message:
Caller:	
Company:	
Phone:	
Email:	
Urgency: Low/Medium/High	Called ☐
Date: Time:	Message:
Caller:	
Company:	
Phone:	
Email:	
Urgency: Low/Medium/High	Called ☐
Date: Time:	Message:
Caller:	
Company:	
Phone:	
Email:	
Urgency: Low/Medium/High	Called ☐

Date: Time:	Message:
Caller:	
Company:	
Phone:	
Email:	
Urgency: Low/Medium/High	Called ☐
Date: Time:	Message:
Caller:	
Company:	
Phone:	
Email:	
Urgency: Low/Medium/High	Called ☐
Date: Time:	Message:
Caller:	
Company:	
Phone:	
Email:	
Urgency: Low/Medium/High	Called ☐
Date: Time:	Message:
Caller:	
Company:	
Phone:	
Email:	
Urgency: Low/Medium/High	Called ☐
Date: Time:	Message:
Caller:	
Company:	
Phone:	
Email:	
Urgency: Low/Medium/High	Called ☐

	Message:
Date: Time:	
Caller:	
Company:	
Phone:	
Email:	
Urgency: Low/Medium/High	Called ☐
Date: Time:	Message:
Caller:	
Company:	
Phone:	
Email:	
Urgency: Low/Medium/High	Called ☐
Date: Time:	Message:
Caller:	
Company:	
Phone:	
Email:	
Urgency: Low/Medium/High	Called ☐
Date: Time:	Message:
Caller:	
Company:	
Phone:	
Email:	
Urgency: Low/Medium/High	Called ☐
Date: Time:	Message:
Caller:	
Company:	
Phone:	
Email:	
Urgency: Low/Medium/High	Called ☐

Date: Time:	Message:
Caller:	
Company:	
Phone:	
Email:	
Urgency: Low/Medium/High	Called ☐
Date: Time:	Message:
Caller:	
Company:	
Phone:	
Email:	
Urgency: Low/Medium/High	Called ☐
Date: Time:	Message:
Caller:	
Company:	
Phone:	
Email:	
Urgency: Low/Medium/High	Called ☐
Date: Time:	Message:
Caller:	
Company:	
Phone:	
Email:	
Urgency: Low/Medium/High	Called ☐
Date: Time:	Message:
Caller:	
Company:	
Phone:	
Email:	
Urgency: Low/Medium/High	Called ☐

Date: Time:	Message:
Caller:	
Company:	
Phone:	
Email:	
Urgency: Low/Medium/High	Called ☐
Date: Time:	Message:
Caller:	
Company:	
Phone:	
Email:	
Urgency: Low/Medium/High	Called ☐
Date: Time:	Message:
Caller:	
Company:	
Phone:	
Email:	
Urgency: Low/Medium/High	Called ☐
Date: Time:	Message:
Caller:	
Company:	
Phone:	
Email:	
Urgency: Low/Medium/High	Called ☐
Date: Time:	Message:
Caller:	
Company:	
Phone:	
Email:	
Urgency: Low/Medium/High	Called ☐

Date: Time:	Message:
Caller:	
Company:	
Phone:	
Email:	
Urgency: Low/Medium/High	Called ☐
Date: Time:	Message:
Caller:	
Company:	
Phone:	
Email:	
Urgency: Low/Medium/High	Called ☐
Date: Time:	Message:
Caller:	
Company:	
Phone:	
Email:	
Urgency: Low/Medium/High	Called ☐
Date: Time:	Message:
Caller:	
Company:	
Phone:	
Email:	
Urgency: Low/Medium/High	Called ☐
Date: Time:	Message:
Caller:	
Company:	
Phone:	
Email:	
Urgency: Low/Medium/High	Called ☐

Date: Time:	Message:
Caller:	
Company:	
Phone:	
Email:	
Urgency: Low/Medium/High	Called ☐
Date: Time:	Message:
Caller:	
Company:	
Phone:	
Email:	
Urgency: Low/Medium/High	Called ☐
Date: Time:	Message:
Caller:	
Company:	
Phone:	
Email:	
Urgency: Low/Medium/High	Called ☐
Date: Time:	Message:
Caller:	
Company:	
Phone:	
Email:	
Urgency: Low/Medium/High	Called ☐
Date: Time:	Message:
Caller:	
Company:	
Phone:	
Email:	
Urgency: Low/Medium/High	Called ☐

	Message:
Date: Time:	
Caller:	
Company:	
Phone:	
Email:	
Urgency: Low/Medium/High	Called ☐
Date: Time:	Message:
Caller:	
Company:	
Phone:	
Email:	
Urgency: Low/Medium/High	Called ☐
Date: Time:	Message:
Caller:	
Company:	
Phone:	
Email:	
Urgency: Low/Medium/High	Called ☐
Date: Time:	Message:
Caller:	
Company:	
Phone:	
Email:	
Urgency: Low/Medium/High	Called ☐
Date: Time:	Message:
Caller:	
Company:	
Phone:	
Email:	
Urgency: Low/Medium/High	Called ☐

Date: Time:	Message:
Caller:	
Company:	
Phone:	
Email:	
Urgency: Low/Medium/High	Called ☐
Date: Time:	Message:
Caller:	
Company:	
Phone:	
Email:	
Urgency: Low/Medium/High	Called ☐
Date: Time:	Message:
Caller:	
Company:	
Phone:	
Email:	
Urgency: Low/Medium/High	Called ☐
Date: Time:	Message:
Caller:	
Company:	
Phone:	
Email:	
Urgency: Low/Medium/High	Called ☐
Date: Time:	Message:
Caller:	
Company:	
Phone:	
Email:	
Urgency: Low/Medium/High	Called ☐

Date: Time:	Message:
Caller:	
Company:	
Phone:	
Email:	
Urgency: Low/Medium/High	Called ☐
Date: Time:	Message:
Caller:	
Company:	
Phone:	
Email:	
Urgency: Low/Medium/High	Called ☐
Date: Time:	Message:
Caller:	
Company:	
Phone:	
Email:	
Urgency: Low/Medium/High	Called ☐
Date: Time:	Message:
Caller:	
Company:	
Phone:	
Email:	
Urgency: Low/Medium/High	Called ☐
Date: Time:	Message:
Caller:	
Company:	
Phone:	
Email:	
Urgency: Low/Medium/High	Called ☐

Date: Time:	Message:
Caller:	
Company:	
Phone:	
Email:	
Urgency: Low/Medium/High	Called ☐
Date: Time:	Message:
Caller:	
Company:	
Phone:	
Email:	
Urgency: Low/Medium/High	Called ☐
Date: Time:	Message:
Caller:	
Company:	
Phone:	
Email:	
Urgency: Low/Medium/High	Called ☐
Date: Time:	Message:
Caller:	
Company:	
Phone:	
Email:	
Urgency: Low/Medium/High	Called ☐
Date: Time:	Message:
Caller:	
Company:	
Phone:	
Email:	
Urgency: Low/Medium/High	Called ☐

Date: Time:	Message:
Caller:	
Company:	
Phone:	
Email:	
Urgency: Low/Medium/High	Called ☐
Date: Time:	Message:
Caller:	
Company:	
Phone:	
Email:	
Urgency: Low/Medium/High	Called ☐
Date: Time:	Message:
Caller:	
Company:	
Phone:	
Email:	
Urgency: Low/Medium/High	Called ☐
Date: Time:	Message:
Caller:	
Company:	
Phone:	
Email:	
Urgency: Low/Medium/High	Called ☐
Date: Time:	Message:
Caller:	
Company:	
Phone:	
Email:	
Urgency: Low/Medium/High	Called ☐

	Message:
Date: Time:	
Caller:	
Company:	
Phone:	
Email:	
Urgency: Low/Medium/High	Called ☐
Date: Time:	Message:
Caller:	
Company:	
Phone:	
Email:	
Urgency: Low/Medium/High	Called ☐
Date: Time:	Message:
Caller:	
Company:	
Phone:	
Email:	
Urgency: Low/Medium/High	Called ☐
Date: Time:	Message:
Caller:	
Company:	
Phone:	
Email:	
Urgency: Low/Medium/High	Called ☐
Date: Time:	Message:
Caller:	
Company:	
Phone:	
Email:	
Urgency: Low/Medium/High	Called ☐

Date: Time:	Message:
Caller:	
Company:	
Phone:	
Email:	
Urgency: Low/Medium/High	Called ☐
Date: Time:	Message:
Caller:	
Company:	
Phone:	
Email:	
Urgency: Low/Medium/High	Called ☐
Date: Time:	Message:
Caller:	
Company:	
Phone:	
Email:	
Urgency: Low/Medium/High	Called ☐
Date: Time:	Message:
Caller:	
Company:	
Phone:	
Email:	
Urgency: Low/Medium/High	Called ☐
Date: Time:	Message:
Caller:	
Company:	
Phone:	
Email:	
Urgency: Low/Medium/High	Called ☐

Date: Time:	Message:
Caller:	
Company:	
Phone:	
Email:	
Urgency: Low/Medium/High	Called ☐
Date: Time:	Message:
Caller:	
Company:	
Phone:	
Email:	
Urgency: Low/Medium/High	Called ☐
Date: Time:	Message:
Caller:	
Company:	
Phone:	
Email:	
Urgency: Low/Medium/High	Called ☐
Date: Time:	Message:
Caller:	
Company:	
Phone:	
Email:	
Urgency: Low/Medium/High	Called ☐
Date: Time:	Message:
Caller:	
Company:	
Phone:	
Email:	
Urgency: Low/Medium/High	Called ☐

Date: Time:	Message:
Caller:	
Company:	
Phone:	
Email:	
Urgency: Low/Medium/High	Called ☐
Date: Time:	Message:
Caller:	
Company:	
Phone:	
Email:	
Urgency: Low/Medium/High	Called ☐
Date: Time:	Message:
Caller:	
Company:	
Phone:	
Email:	
Urgency: Low/Medium/High	Called ☐
Date: Time:	Message:
Caller:	
Company:	
Phone:	
Email:	
Urgency: Low/Medium/High	Called ☐
Date: Time:	Message:
Caller:	
Company:	
Phone:	
Email:	
Urgency: Low/Medium/High	Called ☐

Date: Time:	Message:
Caller:	
Company:	
Phone:	
Email:	
Urgency: Low/Medium/High	Called ☐
Date: Time:	Message:
Caller:	
Company:	
Phone:	
Email:	
Urgency: Low/Medium/High	Called ☐
Date: Time:	Message:
Caller:	
Company:	
Phone:	
Email:	
Urgency: Low/Medium/High	Called ☐
Date: Time:	Message:
Caller:	
Company:	
Phone:	
Email:	
Urgency: Low/Medium/High	Called ☐
Date: Time:	Message:
Caller:	
Company:	
Phone:	
Email:	
Urgency: Low/Medium/High	Called ☐

Date: Time:	Message:
Caller:	
Company:	
Phone:	
Email:	
Urgency: Low/Medium/High	Called ☐
Date: Time:	Message:
Caller:	
Company:	
Phone:	
Email:	
Urgency: Low/Medium/High	Called ☐
Date: Time:	Message:
Caller:	
Company:	
Phone:	
Email:	
Urgency: Low/Medium/High	Called ☐
Date: Time:	Message:
Caller:	
Company:	
Phone:	
Email:	
Urgency: Low/Medium/High	Called ☐
Date: Time:	Message:
Caller:	
Company:	
Phone:	
Email:	
Urgency: Low/Medium/High	Called ☐

Date: Time:	Message:
Caller:	
Company:	
Phone:	
Email:	
Urgency: Low/Medium/High	Called ☐
Date: Time:	Message:
Caller:	
Company:	
Phone:	
Email:	
Urgency: Low/Medium/High	Called ☐
Date: Time:	Message:
Caller:	
Company:	
Phone:	
Email:	
Urgency: Low/Medium/High	Called ☐
Date: Time:	Message:
Caller:	
Company:	
Phone:	
Email:	
Urgency: Low/Medium/High	Called ☐
Date: Time:	Message:
Caller:	
Company:	
Phone:	
Email:	
Urgency: Low/Medium/High	Called ☐

Date: Time:	Message:
Caller:	
Company:	
Phone:	
Email:	
Urgency: Low/Medium/High	Called □
Date: Time:	Message:
Caller:	
Company:	
Phone:	
Email:	
Urgency: Low/Medium/High	Called □
Date: Time:	Message:
Caller:	
Company:	
Phone:	
Email:	
Urgency: Low/Medium/High	Called □
Date: Time:	Message:
Caller:	
Company:	
Phone:	
Email:	
Urgency: Low/Medium/High	Called □
Date: Time:	Message:
Caller:	
Company:	
Phone:	
Email:	
Urgency: Low/Medium/High	Called □

Date: Time:	Message:
Caller:	
Company:	
Phone:	
Email:	
Urgency: Low/Medium/High	Called ☐

Date: Time:	Message:
Caller:	
Company:	
Phone:	
Email:	
Urgency: Low/Medium/High	Called ☐

Date: Time:	Message:
Caller:	
Company:	
Phone:	
Email:	
Urgency: Low/Medium/High	Called ☐

Date: Time:	Message:
Caller:	
Company:	
Phone:	
Email:	
Urgency: Low/Medium/High	Called ☐

Date: Time:	Message:
Caller:	
Company:	
Phone:	
Email:	
Urgency: Low/Medium/High	Called ☐

Date: Time:	Message:
Caller:	
Company:	
Phone:	
Email:	
Urgency: Low/Medium/High	Called ☐
Date: Time:	Message:
Caller:	
Company:	
Phone:	
Email:	
Urgency: Low/Medium/High	Called ☐
Date: Time:	Message:
Caller:	
Company:	
Phone:	
Email:	
Urgency: Low/Medium/High	Called ☐
Date: Time:	Message:
Caller:	
Company:	
Phone:	
Email:	
Urgency: Low/Medium/High	Called ☐
Date: Time:	Message:
Caller:	
Company:	
Phone:	
Email:	
Urgency: Low/Medium/High	Called ☐

Date: Time:	Message:
Caller:	
Company:	
Phone:	
Email:	
Urgency: Low/Medium/High	Called ☐
Date: Time:	Message:
Caller:	
Company:	
Phone:	
Email:	
Urgency: Low/Medium/High	Called ☐
Date: Time:	Message:
Caller:	
Company:	
Phone:	
Email:	
Urgency: Low/Medium/High	Called ☐
Date: Time:	Message:
Caller:	
Company:	
Phone:	
Email:	
Urgency: Low/Medium/High	Called ☐
Date: Time:	Message:
Caller:	
Company:	
Phone:	
Email:	
Urgency: Low/Medium/High	Called ☐

	Message:
Date: Time:	
Caller:	
Company:	
Phone:	
Email:	
Urgency: Low/Medium/High	Called ☐
Date: Time:	Message:
Caller:	
Company:	
Phone:	
Email:	
Urgency: Low/Medium/High	Called ☐
Date: Time:	Message:
Caller:	
Company:	
Phone:	
Email:	
Urgency: Low/Medium/High	Called ☐
Date: Time:	Message:
Caller:	
Company:	
Phone:	
Email:	
Urgency: Low/Medium/High	Called ☐
Date: Time:	Message:
Caller:	
Company:	
Phone:	
Email:	
Urgency: Low/Medium/High	Called ☐

Date: Time:	Message:
Caller:	
Company:	
Phone:	
Email:	
Urgency: Low/Medium/High	Called ☐

Date: Time:	Message:
Caller:	
Company:	
Phone:	
Email:	
Urgency: Low/Medium/High	Called ☐

Date: Time:	Message:
Caller:	
Company:	
Phone:	
Email:	
Urgency: Low/Medium/High	Called ☐

Date: Time:	Message:
Caller:	
Company:	
Phone:	
Email:	
Urgency: Low/Medium/High	Called ☐

Date: Time:	Message:
Caller:	
Company:	
Phone:	
Email:	
Urgency: Low/Medium/High	Called ☐

Date: Time:	Message:
Caller:	
Company:	
Phone:	
Email:	
Urgency: Low/Medium/High	Called ☐
Date: Time:	Message:
Caller:	
Company:	
Phone:	
Email:	
Urgency: Low/Medium/High	Called ☐
Date: Time:	Message:
Caller:	
Company:	
Phone:	
Email:	
Urgency: Low/Medium/High	Called ☐
Date: Time:	Message:
Caller:	
Company:	
Phone:	
Email:	
Urgency: Low/Medium/High	Called ☐
Date: Time:	Message:
Caller:	
Company:	
Phone:	
Email:	
Urgency: Low/Medium/High	Called ☐

Date: Time:	Message:
Caller:	
Company:	
Phone:	
Email:	
Urgency: Low/Medium/High	Called ☐
Date: Time:	Message:
Caller:	
Company:	
Phone:	
Email:	
Urgency: Low/Medium/High	Called ☐
Date: Time:	Message:
Caller:	
Company:	
Phone:	
Email:	
Urgency: Low/Medium/High	Called ☐
Date: Time:	Message:
Caller:	
Company:	
Phone:	
Email:	
Urgency: Low/Medium/High	Called ☐
Date: Time:	Message:
Caller:	
Company:	
Phone:	
Email:	
Urgency: Low/Medium/High	Called ☐

Date: Time:	Message:
Caller:	
Company:	
Phone:	
Email:	
Urgency: Low/Medium/High	Called ☐
Date: Time:	Message:
Caller:	
Company:	
Phone:	
Email:	
Urgency: Low/Medium/High	Called ☐
Date: Time:	Message:
Caller:	
Company:	
Phone:	
Email:	
Urgency: Low/Medium/High	Called ☐
Date: Time:	Message:
Caller:	
Company:	
Phone:	
Email:	
Urgency: Low/Medium/High	Called ☐
Date: Time:	Message:
Caller:	
Company:	
Phone:	
Email:	
Urgency: Low/Medium/High	Called ☐

Date: Time:	Message:
Caller:	
Company:	
Phone:	
Email:	
Urgency: Low/Medium/High	Called ☐
Date: Time:	Message:
Caller:	
Company:	
Phone:	
Email:	
Urgency: Low/Medium/High	Called ☐
Date: Time:	Message:
Caller:	
Company:	
Phone:	
Email:	
Urgency: Low/Medium/High	Called ☐
Date: Time:	Message:
Caller:	
Company:	
Phone:	
Email:	
Urgency: Low/Medium/High	Called ☐
Date: Time:	Message:
Caller:	
Company:	
Phone:	
Email:	
Urgency: Low/Medium/High	Called ☐

Date:　　　　　Time:	Message:
Caller:	
Company:	
Phone:	
Email:	
Urgency: Low/Medium/High	Called ☐
Date:　　　　　Time:	Message:
Caller:	
Company:	
Phone:	
Email:	
Urgency: Low/Medium/High	Called ☐
Date:　　　　　Time:	Message:
Caller:	
Company:	
Phone:	
Email:	
Urgency: Low/Medium/High	Called ☐
Date:　　　　　Time:	Message:
Caller:	
Company:	
Phone:	
Email:	
Urgency: Low/Medium/High	Called ☐
Date:　　　　　Time:	Message:
Caller:	
Company:	
Phone:	
Email:	
Urgency: Low/Medium/High	Called ☐

	Message:
Date: Time:	
Caller:	
Company:	
Phone:	
Email:	
Urgency: Low/Medium/High	Called ☐
Date: Time:	Message:
Caller:	
Company:	
Phone:	
Email:	
Urgency: Low/Medium/High	Called ☐
Date: Time:	Message:
Caller:	
Company:	
Phone:	
Email:	
Urgency: Low/Medium/High	Called ☐
Date: Time:	Message:
Caller:	
Company:	
Phone:	
Email:	
Urgency: Low/Medium/High	Called ☐
Date: Time:	Message:
Caller:	
Company:	
Phone:	
Email:	
Urgency: Low/Medium/High	Called ☐

Date: Time:	Message:
Caller:	
Company:	
Phone:	
Email:	
Urgency: Low/Medium/High	Called ☐
Date: Time:	Message:
Caller:	
Company:	
Phone:	
Email:	
Urgency: Low/Medium/High	Called ☐
Date: Time:	Message:
Caller:	
Company:	
Phone:	
Email:	
Urgency: Low/Medium/High	Called ☐
Date: Time:	Message:
Caller:	
Company:	
Phone:	
Email:	
Urgency: Low/Medium/High	Called ☐
Date: Time:	Message:
Caller:	
Company:	
Phone:	
Email:	
Urgency: Low/Medium/High	Called ☐

Date: Time:	Message:
Caller:	
Company:	
Phone:	
Email:	
Urgency: Low/Medium/High	Called ☐
Date: Time:	Message:
Caller:	
Company:	
Phone:	
Email:	
Urgency: Low/Medium/High	Called ☐
Date: Time:	Message:
Caller:	
Company:	
Phone:	
Email:	
Urgency: Low/Medium/High	Called ☐
Date: Time:	Message:
Caller:	
Company:	
Phone:	
Email:	
Urgency: Low/Medium/High	Called ☐
Date: Time:	Message:
Caller:	
Company:	
Phone:	
Email:	
Urgency: Low/Medium/High	Called ☐

Date:　　　　　Time:	Message:
Caller:	
Company:	
Phone:	
Email:	
Urgency: Low/Medium/High	Called ☐
Date:　　　　　Time:	Message:
Caller:	
Company:	
Phone:	
Email:	
Urgency: Low/Medium/High	Called ☐
Date:　　　　　Time:	Message:
Caller:	
Company:	
Phone:	
Email:	
Urgency: Low/Medium/High	Called ☐
Date:　　　　　Time:	Message:
Caller:	
Company:	
Phone:	
Email:	
Urgency: Low/Medium/High	Called ☐
Date:　　　　　Time:	Message:
Caller:	
Company:	
Phone:	
Email:	
Urgency: Low/Medium/High	Called ☐

	Message:
Date: Time:	
Caller:	
Company:	
Phone:	
Email:	
Urgency: Low/Medium/High	Called ☐
Date: Time:	Message:
Caller:	
Company:	
Phone:	
Email:	
Urgency: Low/Medium/High	Called ☐
Date: Time:	Message:
Caller:	
Company:	
Phone:	
Email:	
Urgency: Low/Medium/High	Called ☐
Date: Time:	Message:
Caller:	
Company:	
Phone:	
Email:	
Urgency: Low/Medium/High	Called ☐
Date: Time:	Message:
Caller:	
Company:	
Phone:	
Email:	
Urgency: Low/Medium/High	Called ☐

Date: Time:	Message:
Caller:	
Company:	
Phone:	
Email:	
Urgency: Low/Medium/High	Called ☐
Date: Time:	Message:
Caller:	
Company:	
Phone:	
Email:	
Urgency: Low/Medium/High	Called ☐
Date: Time:	Message:
Caller:	
Company:	
Phone:	
Email:	
Urgency: Low/Medium/High	Called ☐
Date: Time:	Message:
Caller:	
Company:	
Phone:	
Email:	
Urgency: Low/Medium/High	Called ☐
Date: Time:	Message:
Caller:	
Company:	
Phone:	
Email:	
Urgency: Low/Medium/High	Called ☐

Date: Time:	Message:
Caller:	
Company:	
Phone:	
Email:	
Urgency: Low/Medium/High	Called ☐
Date: Time:	Message:
Caller:	
Company:	
Phone:	
Email:	
Urgency: Low/Medium/High	Called ☐
Date: Time:	Message:
Caller:	
Company:	
Phone:	
Email:	
Urgency: Low/Medium/High	Called ☐
Date: Time:	Message:
Caller:	
Company:	
Phone:	
Email:	
Urgency: Low/Medium/High	Called ☐
Date: Time:	Message:
Caller:	
Company:	
Phone:	
Email:	
Urgency: Low/Medium/High	Called ☐

Date: Time:	Message:
Caller:	
Company:	
Phone:	
Email:	
Urgency: Low/Medium/High	Called ☐
Date: Time:	Message:
Caller:	
Company:	
Phone:	
Email:	
Urgency: Low/Medium/High	Called ☐
Date: Time:	Message:
Caller:	
Company:	
Phone:	
Email:	
Urgency: Low/Medium/High	Called ☐
Date: Time:	Message:
Caller:	
Company:	
Phone:	
Email:	
Urgency: Low/Medium/High	Called ☐
Date: Time:	Message:
Caller:	
Company:	
Phone:	
Email:	
Urgency: Low/Medium/High	Called ☐

	Message:
Date: Time:	
Caller:	
Company:	
Phone:	
Email:	
Urgency: Low/Medium/High	Called ☐
Date: Time:	Message:
Caller:	
Company:	
Phone:	
Email:	
Urgency: Low/Medium/High	Called ☐
Date: Time:	Message:
Caller:	
Company:	
Phone:	
Email:	
Urgency: Low/Medium/High	Called ☐
Date: Time:	Message:
Caller:	
Company:	
Phone:	
Email:	
Urgency: Low/Medium/High	Called ☐
Date: Time:	Message:
Caller:	
Company:	
Phone:	
Email:	
Urgency: Low/Medium/High	Called ☐

Printed in Great Britain
by Amazon